POST CARD S TALK

Linda Granfield

Illustrated by
Mark Thurman

Pembroke Publishers Limited

©1998 Linda Granfield, text
©1998 Mark Thurman, illustration

Pembroke Publishers
538 Hood Road
Markham, Ontario L3R 3K9 Canada

Canadian Cataloguing in Publication Data

Granfield, Linda
  Postcards talk

ISBN 1-55138-032-3 (hc)
ISBN 1-55138-033-1 (pbk)

1. Postcards – Juvenile literature.   2. Handicraft –
Juvenile literature.   I. Thurman, Mark, 1948-   .

NC1872.G73 1997   j741.68'3   C97-931060-1

Design: John Zehethofer
Typesetting: Jay Tee Graphics

Printed and bound in Canada
9 8 7 6 5 4 3 2 1

· POSTCARDS ARE FROM PRIVATE COLLECTIONS ·

Contents

Casa Loma, Toronto, Canada

Wish You Were Here!

For more than one hundred years, people have been sending messages on postcards. Millions of them have been printed on paper, leather, wood and even metal. They've been mailed to destinations all over the world and saved as souvenirs in special scrapbook albums.

Want to join the fun? You can use postcards to
- keep in touch with pen-pals
- send a quick note to your grandparents
- celebrate birthdays and holidays
- remember a family vacation
- share camp experiences with friends

A supply of your postcard originals (or some blank postcards and pencil crayons) makes a great gift!

How to Make Your Own Postcards

Trace or photocopy this postcard outline. Find some paper that is about as thick as the cover of this book. Use the pattern to cut out as many blank cards from the thick paper as you want. It's time to have your say . . . with postcards!

Postcards Old and New

Postcards are older than you might think. Early cards were printed in Europe in the 1860s and were used for advertising businesses. By 1900, photographic equipment had improved, and the pictures on postcards were more realistic and detailed.

As working folk began to have more leisure time they travelled more, locally and around the world. And they purchased souvenirs, including postcards, wherever they went.

Today, there are electronic postcards available on the Internet. You can visit sites around the world, trade cards with fellow collectors and view some of the latest designs.

Exploring Art—The Illustrated Side

A hundred years ago, people collected postcards for the colorful illustrations. Some families even wallpapered rooms with them. A postcard was an inexpensive way to have art on your walls.

How Will *You* Decorate *Your* Postcards?

Now is the time to experiment with some new art techniques or to practise methods you already use. Here are some ideas to help you.

Photographs

Trim a snapshot of a person or place, and glue it to the postcard. Add stickers. Or paint a colorful border.

Cartoons

Since long ago, postcard artists have drawn caricatures, or cartoons, of people. Give a friend a laugh! Draw a funny portrait of yourself or of the person who is going to receive the card.

Silhouettes

People cut out black shadow shapes of people, or silhouettes, long before they had cameras. Who is the person on the postcard? Create a mystery!

Collage

Gather photos, magazine illustrations, labels, stars, whatever is around your home. Play with the colors and shapes until you have an arrangement you like. Glue down the collage pieces. (Be sure all the edges are glued down so they won't tear off in the mail. You might want to laminate collage postcards or mail them in an envelope.)

Paint Techniques

Use watercolors or poster paints to spatter, sponge or comb designs on the postcard. When dry, the painted card makes a great background for photo or silhouette postcards. Stencils, rubber stamps and thumb prints also make interesting postcard designs.

Exaggeration

Make an exaggeration card. That's a postcard where items are drawn out of proportion, just for fun. For example, the fish caught might be two times the size of the person who caught it.

How to Laminate Your Postcards

If your postcard needs a protective covering, simply cut a piece of clear, self-adhesive vinyl slightly larger than your card. Peel off the paper backing and gently centre the front of the postcard on the vinyl. Fold the edges to the back of the postcard. Turn the card over and, using your fingers, press out any air pockets that may be on the front.

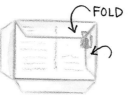

FOLD

Travel Cards

Whether you buy them or make your own, postcards are a great record of your vacation trip. Each year, new postcard designs and views are produced. It's said that there are at least 5,000 different postcard views of Niagara Falls available!

Fun with Travel Cards

- Mail a postcard to a friend. You can share your new experiences and stay in touch.
- Make an album (see page 29) and put postcards in it. You'll have something to bring back memories for years to come.
- Collect cards of your hometown. Or make a postcard of your city for someone who has never been there.
- Send a pen-pal a postcard of your house, even your bedroom (before and after you cleaned it up!).
- Invent an imaginary place. Create a map postcard of that place. Add buildings or the inhabitants of the fantasy spot. How many details can you include?

Pictures of tourist attractions, buildings and landscapes are traditionally called view cards. What place in your neighborhood would make an interesting view card?

11

Special Occasion Cards

Unusual Holidays

Old postcards that celebrate holidays are considered valuable by card collectors. Here's your chance to make postcards that celebrate holidays that may never before have been illustrated on cards, like Crayfish Day (August 8) or Groundhog Day (February 2)!

Special Events

You can make cards to celebrate the birthdays or graduations of friends and relatives. Maybe your grandparents have retired, or your friend is moving into a new house. Did your cousin win a baseball trophy? Send a personalized postcard with your creative "Congratulations" message.

GROUNDHOG DAY!

CRAYFISH DAY!

NOSTRIL DAY!

BAD BREATH DAY!

AUSTRALIAN RETURN TO SENDER POSTCARD

Traditional Holidays

Celebrate important traditional and religious holidays, like Chanukah, Christmas, Kwanzaa or Diwali by sending specially designed postcards that highlight the symbols of the holiday. Use some glitter or metallic markers to give extra sparkle to your cards.

A Postcard Calendar

For each month create a different design. Photocopy the pages of a calendar (you'll have to reduce the page size so each month will fit on a card) and glue one month on each postcard.

   If the calendar is a gift, write a special message on the back of each card. Package the twelve cards with a clear, plastic photo holder that will display the current month.

13

Having Your Say—The Written Side

Until 1907, it was illegal to write anything except the address on the back of a postcard. A picture was printed on the front of the card, and only a very small space was left there for someone to write a very brief message. "A huge puddle, By Jove," a tourist wrote on the front of a postcard when he visited Niagara Falls in 1906. (And that's the complete message!)

Modern postcards give us a much larger space to write in, but your message still needs to be brief. How will you communicate a message on your postcards?

Hidden Messages

People have always worried about strangers reading their postcard messages since there isn't an envelope to cover them. Creative card writers have found ways to communicate—and keep their messages private. You might try one of the following.

Secret Codes

Create a code that only you and your friends or family will understand. Use shapes or numbers, for instance. (Just be sure you and your receiver both know what the shapes mean, or else your message will be a secret forever!)

Backwards Writing

With a bit of practice, you can print your letters and words backwards. When the postcard arrives, your friend will have to hold the card up to a mirror. Then the message can be clearly read.

In the 1400s, the great inventor and artist Leonardo da Vinci filled his scientific notebooks with backwards writing so that enemies could not understand his work.

Circular Writing

Start in the middle of a blank postcard. Write "Dear John," and turn the card in a circular motion as you continue to write the message. When your friend turns the card while reading it, everything will make sense. But anyone just glancing at the message won't be able to understand it.

You can practise circular writing on a piece of paper and later work in smaller print on a postcard.

Cross-Writing

In the 1700s, paper was too expensive to waste on envelopes that would be thrown away, so people used every area of a sheet of writing paper, but they wrote only on one side. When the paper was folded, the blank side became an envelope.

Cross-writing meant that more could be said on one side of the paper. You can cross-write on a postcard space, too, and say plenty that can't be read when glanced at.

Write your message the way you want in the space allowed. When you run out of space, turn the card and write across the lines already there. You've doubled your writing space!

Playing with Words

You can play with words and their meanings on postcards. An old postcard said, "I knead the dough," and showed someone at work kneading bread. Another said, "You're the 🍎 of my eye," and showed a character with an apple-head. Here are some ways to play with words on your postcards.

A Rebus

Make a rebus postcard, with pictures representing words, or parts of words. (Example: an eye for "I," the numeral 4 for "for," a heart for "love.")

Jokes and Riddles

Try writing jokes. Put the question part of a riddle on the front with a picture. Put the answer on the back.

Rhymes

Make rhyming messages to advertise for a summer job baby-sitting, gardening or pet-minding.

Slang

Use the slang from camp, school or even your part of the country. The writing, matched with the picture on the front, will tell the receiver about you and where you live.

Hello Central give me the MOON

In 1900, a Norwegian fellow finished writing a 46,000 word novel on *one* postcard. The job took him four years!

Write On!

If you have some old postcards around your house, investigate how the messages were written—and what with!

Old-fashioned pens didn't come filled with ink as they do now. You needed a bottle of ink and a pen to dip into it, over and over again. If you look at an old postcard sent around 1900, you can see ink blotches in the message because it was difficult for the writer to apply pressure evenly on the pen in order to avoid a mess.

Pocket pens, like the ones you use, were invented because of the inconvenience of carrying writing supplies. Travellers and soldiers, for instance, couldn't carry pens, ink bottles, nibs and blotters in their pockets, and carrying cases were awkward. Later inventions included the ball-point pen, felt-tipped markers and neon pencils.

Curlicues

Some handwriting from the past is ornate. Capital letters have long, fancy tails, and addresses are written with flourishes. Around 1900, when you could write only a person's name and address on the back of the card, there was plenty of room for such artistic work.

You can try some calligraphy, or fancy writing, on your own postcards. There are even special calligraphic felt-tipped pens available, so you won't need a bottle of ink and a quill pen!

18

Writing Imaginatively

Can't think of anything to write on your postcard? Why not make up a story to go with the picture you've drawn? Try making a folding postcard (see pages 22/23), with a "chapter" on each card.

Use Postcards from the Past

If you have some old postcards around the house, why not write a story based on the pictures? The cards can provide the setting for your story, like a city hall, a school, a market that was torn down. The people on the cards can be your characters.

Write a Mystery Story

Or maybe you want to create everything in the story yourself. Let's say you'd like to write a postcard mystery. You can write the story, and give a new clue on each card. (The clue might be found on the picture side, or on the written side. Whether you use words or pictures, make sure your clues help tell your story.) On the last card, the mystery will be solved!

Better yet, don't reveal the final solution! Keep your friend waiting for the next installment. Mail the next folding postcard a few days later.

How about a Never-ending Mystery???

Or . . . send the first folding postcard, with the mystery unsolved, to a friend. Ask your friend to make *another* folding postcard that continues the mystery. And so on. Back and forth, from friend to friend. Maybe ten folding postcards later, the mystery will be solved!

UPON MY SOLE I'M GLAD I CAME HERE

You are the

MY POOR OLD FEET APPRECIATE IT.
THE OTHER ONE'S JUST AS PLEASED AS THIS!

of my eye

FOLD

Thanksgiving
Greeting

How to Make a Folding Postcard

Trace or photocopy the folding postcard
pattern on these pages and cut it out.
Now use the cut-out as a template to
trace the pattern on lightweight paper
(like the pages of this book). This will be
the cover of your folding postcard.

Using the single postcard pattern on
page 5, trace a series of joined postcards.
Cut the strip of cards and fold it
accordion-style. Draw pictures on the
front sides of the cards, and messages or
stories on the back. Laminate the cover if
you'd like. Tape the accordion to the
inside of the cover, cut the slot and insert
the tab. If necessary, tape the tab shut.
(Be sure to find out how much postage is
required for this heavier postcard.)

23

Reaching into the Past, Present and Future

Old postcards show us how people lived long ago. We see how they dressed, where they lived, what they did to have fun. Famous people appeared on postcards the way rock musicians and movie stars do now. Sometimes the postcards were the only pin-up photos the fans ever saw.

During wartime, postcards provided the world with battle scenes, and cards with patriotic messages were used to raise funds.

Today, costume and set designers use old postcards to create authentic costumes and sets for the movies and plays you see.

Make Your Own Time Capsule

Imagine for a moment that it's the year 2100 and a movie is being made about the lives of young people around the year 2000. Your postcards might be used to learn about clothing, music and games in the "good old days." Design postcards that communicate the "stars" of today, the fashions, the behavior, your pet peeves. How about the inside of a video store or a fast-food outlet?

Special Events

Consider a special event from your lifetime, like the birth of a baby brother or sister, or the day your team won the championship, and design a card to remember the occasion. Imagine how *you* looked on the day you were born, and draw a self-portrait postcard!

PAST

What's New?

Exciting events have been the subjects of postcard designs since they were first made. For example, when Halley's Comet flew past the earth in 1910 (during the heyday of the postcard), manufacturers hurried to repeat the comet's design on cards. The great comet appeared on postcards advertising soap, thread and baking powder. Lovers, children, pets—everyone on the postcards sat by the light of the comet. (And no one worried about the scientific accuracy of the designs!)

New-fangled inventions appeared on postcards, too. Some showed early-model telephones and typewriters. Back then these items were considered very modern and stylish. (Imagine a postcard with the latest model of personal computer, or lap-top.)

Amazing Inventions

Can you create some inventions-of-the-future? What shapes will food have in the future? What will a car look like in 2050?

Planetary Postcards

Perhaps you can imagine a fantasy natural wonder in the universe. Or some creatures that will live on another planet when you arrive there.

Incredible Discoveries

And how about today's events? Halley's Comet last appeared in 1986 (it comes back every 76 years), but there are plenty of current topics to incorporate in your original postcards: a new scientific discovery, a person who's uncovered an ancient civilization, a new interpretation of an old topic (like a newly discovered dinosaur).

Collecting Postcards

Once you begin finding and keeping old postcards, or making and using your original designs, you've become a "deltiologist" (pronounced DEL-tee-ol-o-gist), or a postcard collector! You'll want to keep the postcards your friends send and the old cards you've found in a special place . . . like a postcard album.

DELTIOLOGISTS
A BUNCH OF **"WILD"** CARD COLLECTORS.

·POSTCARD·

KOALA A VE

KOALA - BACKVIEW
HOLDING A POSTCARD

KOALA - FRONTVIEW
HOLDING A POSTCARD

In the 1800s, some animals, like Australia's koalas, might never be seen "in the flesh" by people in Europe. A postcard was one way of introducing "new" animals to the rest of the world.

In the early 1900s, a family's postcard album was a prized possession. Painted, or decorated with fancy velvet or embroidered covers, it was usually kept in the parlor, or living room, and was eagerly shown to visitors who politely "oohed" and "aahed" over the contents.

A Postcard Album

You will need:
  heavy paper, like the cover of this book
    drawings, magazine cut-outs,
    stickers, etc.
  construction paper
  scissors
  clear self-adhesive vinyl
  a hole punch
  ribbon, wool or a shoelace
  package of black corner stickers (found
    in photo or stamp shops)
  white felt-tipped marker pen

1. Cut the heavy paper to make front and
   back covers whatever size you'd like.
2. Decorate the covers with drawings,
   cut-outs, stencils, whatever you'd like.
3. Laminate the covers, following the
   instructions given for laminating the
   postcards (page 9).
4. Punch three holes in the left side of the
   covers.
5. Cut sheets of construction paper for
   your inside pages. Punch holes to
   match those on the covers.
6. Put the sheets between the two covers.
   Lace the ribbon, wool or shoelace
   through all the layers and fasten.
7. Attach your postcards to the pages
   with the corner stickers.
8. Use a white marker pen to write
   descriptions, names or dates under the
   postcards.

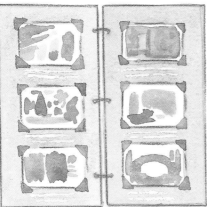

Looking at Stamps

Any deltiologist who also happens to be a philatelist (pronounced fih-LAT-a-list), or stamp collector, will be excited by the many different stamps found on old postcards, and on the cards they exchange with their friends. Famous people, flowers, animals and historical events have appeared on the stamps.

Do Some Detective Work

Borrow a stamp collector's guidebook from your local library, set up a work station with a strong light and a magnifying glass, and start investigating.

Keep a blank notebook nearby so you can jot down any interesting notes, or sketch the different designs and colors.

Design Your Own Stamp

Design a stamp yourself. What important personality or event would you honor if you designed a stamp? (Remember: you can't use your own stamp in place of an official postage stamp.)

Stamp Lingo

The world of stamps has its own language. Here is some information that will help you enjoy investigating stamps.

The **postal marking**, or postmark, shows where and when the mail was sent and includes the cancellation. You'll find different shapes: square, circle, double or single circle, and more.

The **cancellation mark** is the part of the postal mark that covers the stamp so it can't be used again.

STAMP IN THE NORMAL POSITION MEANT "WRITE SOON."

KING'S HEAD TILTED TO THE RIGHT MEANT "THINKING OF YOU."

During the First World War, there was a "language of stamps." The angle of the stamp meant different things to the friend who received the postcard.

So, if you turn the stamp a certain way on your postcard, *and* write in a secret code, the postcard you send really will be private and full of meaning!

EAD TILTED TO THE LEFT EANT "ANSWER AT ONCE."

AN UPSIDE DOWN STAMP MEANT "DO YOU REMEMBER ME?"

31

DEAR
POSTCARD
CREATORS

You've designed, written, addressed, and stamped your postcards. All that's left to do is mail them. And start making more!

DEAR MOM,
CAMP IS OKAY, THE
FOOD STINKS!!
IT RAINS EVERY
DAY. MY COUNSELLOR
HAS DANDRUFF.
YOU SAID
TO WRITE.
LOVE
OMAR

MRS. STONE,
CONCRETE DR.,
NEW YORK,
NEW YORK,
10036
USA

DEAR
BUTTERCUP,
WISH YOU
WERE
HERE.
XOX

MS. FLEUR,
10 BOTANY AVE,
MONTREAL,
QUEBEC

RAVI SINGH,
14 ALDER AVE,
APT. C,
ETOBICOKE,
ONTARIO,
M9C 4G6

DEAR RAVI,
THANKYOU FOR YOUR
LAST POSTCARD! IT
WAS FUN TO DECODE
YOUR MESSAGE.
SEE IF YOU CAN
FIGURE THIS ONE
OUT. YKID 2LKOH2 LI 2TKD2!
YOUR FRIEND
DAN

BEST
WISHES

DEAR RESIDENTS,
CELEBRATE
EARTH
DAY!
EVERY
INHABITANT
OF
THE
PLANET
TO:

APRIL 22

COMING
SOON —
(FROM ZYDECO)
AN OUT OF THIS
WORLD
BAND ·
IRIS AND THE
STRING BEANS

RESERVE
YOUR
TICKETS
NOW!

32